GIGGLE FIT

Super Knock-Knocks

Charles Keller

Illustrated by Steve Harpster

Sterling Publishing Co., Inc. New York

Library of Congress Cataloging-in-Publication Data Available

10   9   8   7   6   5   4   3   2   1

Published in paperback in 2006 by Sterling Publishing Co., Inc.
387 Park Avenue South, New York, N.Y. 10016
© 2003 by Charles Keller
Excerpted from *Little Giant Book of Knock-Knocks* © 1997;
Best Knock-Knock Book Ever © 2000;
Kids' Funniest Knock-Knocks © 2000 all by Charles Keller.
Distributed in Canada by Sterling Publishing
c/o Canadian Manda Group, 165 Dufferin Street
Toronto, Ontario, Canada M6K 3H6
Distributed in the United Kingdom by GMC Distribution Services,
Castle Place, 166 High Street, Lewes, East Sussex, England BN7 1XU
Distributed in Australia by Capricorn Link (Australia) Pty. Ltd.
P.O. Box 704, Windsor, NSW 2756 Australia

Sterling ISBN-13: 978-1-4027-0863-3 Hardcover
        ISBN-10: 1-4027-0863-7

        ISBN-13: 978-1-4027-2772-6 Paperback
        ISBN-10: 1-4027-2772-0

For information about custom editions, special sales, premium and
corporate purchases, please contact Sterling Special Sales
Department at 800-805-5489 or specialsales@sterlingpub.com.

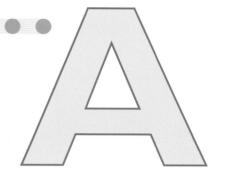

Knock-Knock.
Who's there?
A-1.
A-1 who?
A-1 to know.

Knock-Knock.
Who's there?
Abner.
Abner who?
Abner-cadabra!

Knock-Knock.
Who's there?
Alfie.
Alfie who?
Alfie you later!

Knock-Knock.
  Who's there?
Alibi.
  Alibi who?
Alibi you ice cream.

Knock-Knock.
  Who's there?
Alistair.
  Alistair who?
**Alistair at the TV until
I fall asleep.**

Knock-Knock.
  Who's there?
Alfreda.
  Alfreda who?
Alfreda the dark.

Knock-Knock.
Who's there?
Alpha.
Alpha who?
Alpha one and one for all!

Knock-Knock.
Who's there?
Amarillo.
Amarillo who?
Amarillo fashioned girl.

Knock-Knock.
Who's there?
Amusing.
Amusing who?
Amusing the phone right now.

Knock-Knock.
   Who's there?
Avenue.
   Avenue who?
Avenue baby sister?

Knock-Knock.
   Who's there?
Avoid.
   Avoid who?
Avoid this joke before!

Knock-Knock.
   Who's there?
Augusta.
   Augusta who?
Augusta wind blew my hat off.

Knock-Knock.
Who's there?
Bacon.
Bacon who?
Bacon your pardon.

Knock-Knock.
Who's there?
Beacon.
Beacon who?
Beacon and eggs for breakfast.

Knock-Knock.
Who's there?
Beagles.
Beagles who?
Beagles and cream cheese.

Knock-Knock.
Who's there?
Beach.
Beach who?
Knock-Knock.
Who's there?
Beach.
Beach who?
Knock-Knock.
Who's there?
Beach.
Beach who?
Knock-Knock.
Who's there?
Shore.
Shore who?
Shore glad I didn't say Beach again, aren't you?

Knock-Knock.
  Who's there?
Beets.
  Beets who?
Beets me. I forgot my name.

Knock-Knock.
  Who's there?
Ben.
  Ben who?
Ben knocking so long my hand hurts.

Knock-Knock.
  Who's there?
Ben and Don.
  Ben and Don who?
Ben there, Don that.

Knock-Knock.
  Who's there?
Bella.
  Bella who?
Bella the door isn't working.

Knock-Knock.
   Who's there?
Beth.
   Beth who?
Beth you can't guess.

Knock-Knock.
   Who's there?
Bess.
   Bess who?
Bess of luck.

Knock-Knock.
   Who's there?
Blast.
   Blast who?
Blast chance to open the door!

Knock-Knock.
  Who's there?
Butter.
  Butter who?
Butter late than never.

Knock-Knock.
  Who's there?
Butcher.
  Butcher who?
Butcher money where your mouth is.

Knock-Knock.
  Who's there?
Boris.
  Boris who?
Boris with one more of your stories.

Knock-Knock.
  Who's there?
Canoe.
  Canoe who?
Canoe help me with my homework?

Knock-Knock.
  Who's there?
Cargo.
  Cargo who?
Cargo "Vroom, vroom!"

Knock-Knock.
  Who's there?
Cattle.
  Cattle who?
Cattle screech if you step on its tail.

Knock-Knock.
   Who's there?
Colleen.
   Colleen who?
Colleen up your room.

Knock-Knock.
   Who's there?
Chicken.
   Chicken who?
Chicken up on you.

Knock-Knock.
   Who's there?
Cohen.
   Cohen who?
Cohen around in circles.

Knock-Knock.
   Who's there?
Clark Kent.
   Clark Kent who?
**Clark Kent come,
he's sick.**

Knock-Knock.
 Who's there?
Congo.
 Congo who?
Congo on like this.

Knock-Knock.
 Who's there?
Cotton.
 Cotton who?
Cotton trouble again!

Knock-Knock.
 Who's there?
Cruise.
 Cruise who?
"Cruise afraid of the Big Bad Wolf?"

Knock-Knock.
Who's there?
Denise.
Denise who?
Denise is de sister of de nephew.

Knock-Knock.
Who's there?
Dewey.
Dewey who?
Dewey have to wait out here all day?

Knock-Knock.
Who's there?
Dinosaur.
Dinosaur who?
Dinosaur because he stubbed his toe.

Knock-Knock.
Who's there?
Doug.
Doug who?
Doug a hole on your doorstep.

Knock-Knock.
Who's there?
Donna.
Donna who?
Donna tell me it's bedtime!

Knock-Knock.
Who's there?
Dots.
Dots who?
Dots for me to know and you to find out.

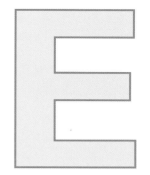

Knock-Knock.
  Who's there?
E.T.
  E.T. who?
**E.T. your food
before it gets cold.**

Knock-Knock.
  Who's there?
Event.
  Event who?
Event that-a-way.

Knock-Knock.
  Who's there?
Emil.
  Emil who?
Emil fit for a king.

F

Knock-Knock.
Who's there?
Furs.
Furs who?
Furs come first served.

Knock-Knock.
Who's there?
Flossie.
Flossie who?
Flossie your teeth.

Knock-Knock.
Who's there?
Fletcher.
Fletcher who?
Fletcher hair down.

18

Knock-Knock
  Who's there?
Gladys.
  Gladys who?
Gladys Friday!

Knock-Knock
  Who's there?
Gnome.
  Gnome who?
Gnome sweet gnome!

Knock-Knock.
  Who's there?
Gwen.
  Gwen who?
Gwen it rains it pours.

Knock-Knock.
  Who's there?
Gruesome.
  Gruesome who?
Gruesome tomatoes in my garden.

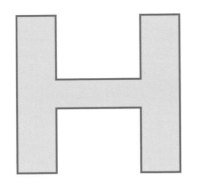

Knock-Knock.
Who's there?
Habit.
Habit who?
Habit your way.

Knock-Knock.
Who's there?
Hannah.
Hannah who?
Hannah me some bubble gum.

Knock-Knock.
Who's there?
Havana.
Havana who?
Havana go home!

20

Knock-Knock.
  Who's there?
Hive.
  Hive who?
Hive got a crush on you.

Knock-Knock.
  Who's there?
Hopi.
  Hopi who?
Hopi new year!

Knock-Knock.
  Who's there?
Honeybee.
  Honeybee who?
Honeybee nice and open the door.

Knock-Knock.
  Who's there?
Ice cream.
  Ice cream who?
Ice cream for you to open the door.

Knock-Knock.
  Who's there?
Ima.
  Ima who?
Ima waiting for you to come out and play.

Knock-Knock.
  Who's there?
Ilona.
  Ilona who?
Ilona you my bike — now give it back!

Knock-Knock.
    Who's there?
Jamaica.
    Jamaica who?
Jamaica fool of yourself again?

Knock-Knock.
    Who's there?
Joel.
    Joel who?
"Joel Macdonald had a farm."

Knock-Knock.
    Who's there?
Jimmy.
    Jimmy who?
Jimmy a raise in my allowance.

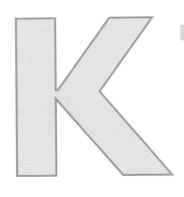

Knock-Knock.
    Who's there?
Kitten.
    Kitten who?
Kitten caboodle.

Knock-Knock.
    Who's there?
Kelp.
    Kelp who?
Kelp yourself to the French fries.

Knock-Knock.
    Who's there?
Kitchen, kitchen.
    Kitchen, kitchen who?
Don't do that, I'm ticklish.

Knock-Knock.
Who's there?
Lena.
Lena who?
Lena little closer and I'll tell you a secret.

Knock-Knock.
Who's there?
Lass.
Lass who?
Lass one home is a rotten egg.

Knock-Knock.
Who's there?
Leif.
Leif who?
Leif me alone.

Knock-Knock.
    Who's there?
Llama.
    Llama who?
Llama bit lost. Can you point the way to the North Pole?

Knock-Knock.
    Who's there?
Lionel.
    Lionel who?
Lionel roar if it's hungry.

Knock-Knock.
    Who's there?
Lux.
    Lux who?
Lux like rain. Let me in!

Knock-Knock.
   Who's there?
Maya.
   Maya who?
Maya big for your age.

Knock-Knock.
   Who's there?
Mary Hannah.
   Mary Hannah who?
Mary Hannah little lamb.

Knock-Knock.
   Who's there?
Mischa.
   Mischa who?
Mischa since you've been away.

Knock-Knock.
  Who's there?
Moose.
  Moose who?
Moose be something I ate.

Knock-Knock.
  Who's there?
Myer.
  Myer who?
Myer in a bad mood today.

Knock-Knock.
  Who's there?
Mustache.
  Mustache who?
Mustache — I'm in a hurry.

Knock-Knock.
Who's there?
Needle.
Needle who?
Needle the help I can get.

Knock-Knock.
Who's there?
Never-Never Land.
Never-Never Land who?
Never-Never Land money to a stranger.

Knock-Knock.
Who's there?
Noah.
Noah who?
Noah-body here but me.

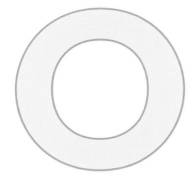

Knock-Knock.
Who's there?
Omelet.
Omelet who?
**Omelet smarter than
I look.**

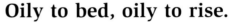

Knock-Knock.
Who's there?
Omar.
Omar who?
**Omar feet are sore. Can
I come in and rest?**

Knock-Knock.
Who's there?
Oily.
Oily who?
Oily to bed, oily to rise.

Knock-Knock.
Who's there?
Oprah.
Oprah who?
Oprah the rainbow...

Knock-Knock.
Who's there?
Orange.
Orange who?
Orange you going to open the door?

Knock-Knock.
Who's there?
Owl.
Owl who?
Owl be seeing you.

Knock-Knock.
Who's there?
Otis.
Otis who?
Otis is a great day for a picnic.

Knock-Knock.
Who's there?
Papaya.
Papaya who?
Papaya the Sailor Man.

Knock-Knock.
Who's there?
Panther.
Panther who?
Panther in the wash, so I wore my shorts.

Knock-Knock.
Who's there?
Peephole.
Peephole who?
Peephole say you're a nice guy.

Knock-Knock.

Who's there?

Police.

Police who?

Police don't talk about me when I'm gone.

Knock-Knock.

Who's there?

Pizza.

Pizza who?

Pizza that apple pie would be good.

Knock-Knock.

Who's there?

Pencil.

Pencil who?

Pencil fall down if you don't wear a belt.

Knock-Knock.
  Who's there?
Quebec.
  Quebec who?
Quebec to the drawing board.

Knock-Knock.
  Who's there?
Quiche.
  Quiche who?
Quiche me, you fool!

Knock-Knock.
  Who's there?
Queen.
  Queen who?
Queen up your room.

Knock-Knock.
Who's there?
Rough.
Rough who?
Rough. Rough. This is your dog speaking...

Knock-Knock.
Who's there?
Raisin.
Raisin who?
Raisin the roof!

Knock-Knock.
 Who's there?
Russia.
 Russia who?
Russia large pizza to this address.

Knock-Knock.
 Who's there?
Radio.
 Radio who?
Radio not, here I come!

Knock-Knock.
   Who's there?
Seymour.
   Seymour who?
Seymour of your friends if you'd open the door once in a while.

Knock-Knock.
   Who's there?
Sanitize.
   Sanitize who?
Sanitize his reindeer to the sleigh.

Knock-Knock.
   Who's there?
Sahara.
   Sahara who?
Sahara you today?

Knock-Knock.
Who's there?
Sheila.
Sheila who?
"Sheila be comin' round the mountain when she comes..."

Knock-Knock.
Who's there?
Sir.
Sir who?
Sir–PRIZE!

Knock-Knock.
Who's there?
Snake.
Snake who?
"Snake me out to the ball game..."

Knock-Knock.
　Who's there?
Sven.
　Sven who?
Sven will you ever learn?

Knock-Knock.
　Who's there?
Sue.
　Sue who?
Don't ask me, I'm not a lawyer.

Knock-Knock.
　Who's there?
Swatter.
　Swatter who?
Swatter you waiting for?

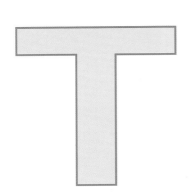

T

Knock-Knock.
Who's there?
Tacoma.
Tacoma who?
**Tacoma your hair —
it's a mess.**

Knock-Knock.
Who's there?
Tamara.
Tamara who?
Tamara is another day.

Knock-Knock.
Who's there?
Taiwan.
Taiwan who?
Taiwan to be happy.

Knock-Knock.
Who's there?
Ticket.
Ticket who?
Ticket or leave it.

Knock-Knock.
Who's there?
Titan.
Titan who?
Titan your seat belt!

Knock-Knock.
Who's there?
Tom Sawyer.
Tom Sawyer who?
Tom Sawyer underwear.

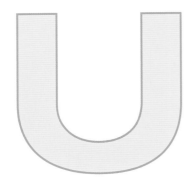

Knock-Knock.
   Who's there?
Utica.
   Utica who?
Utica words right out of my mouth.

Knock-Knock.
   Who's there?
U-Turn.
   U-turn who?
U-Turn off the doorbell?

Knock-Knock.
   Who's there?
Uniform.
   Uniform who?
Uniform a straight line and stand at attention.

Knock-Knock.
Who's there?
Viper.
Viper who?
Viper your hands, they're all wet.

Knock-Knock.
Who's there?
Viola.
Viola who?
Viola fuss? I'm only five minutes late.

Knock-Knock.
Who's there?
Vera.
Vera who?
Vera the cupcakes?

W

Knock-Knock.
 Who's there?
Wooden shoe.
 Wooden shoe who?
**Wooden shoe like to go out
for a walk?**

Knock-Knock.
 Who's there?
Wilma.
 Wilma who?
**Wilma parrot ever
speak?**

Knock-Knock.
 Who's there?
Window.
 Window who?
Window we eat?

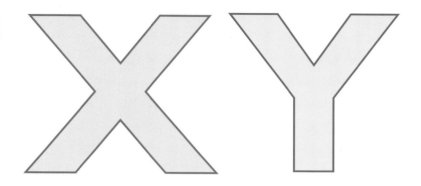

XY

Knock-Knock.
Who's there?
Xylophone.
Xylophone who?
Xylophone and call me.

Knock-Knock.
Who's there?
Yoda.
Yoda who?
Yoda best!

Knock-Knock.
Who's there?
Yuko.
Yuko who?
Yuko your way, I'll go mine.

Knock-Knock.
Who's there?
Yuma.
Yuma who?
Yuma best friend.

Knock-Knock.
Who's there?
Zookeeper.
Zookeeper who?
Zookeeper your shirt on!

Knock-Knock.
Who's there?
Zenda.
Zenda who?
**Zenda walls came
tumbling down.**

Knock-Knock.
Who's there?
Zys.
Zys who?
Zys is the end of the book!

INDEX